THE SPECTACULAR SCIENCE OF BUILDINGS

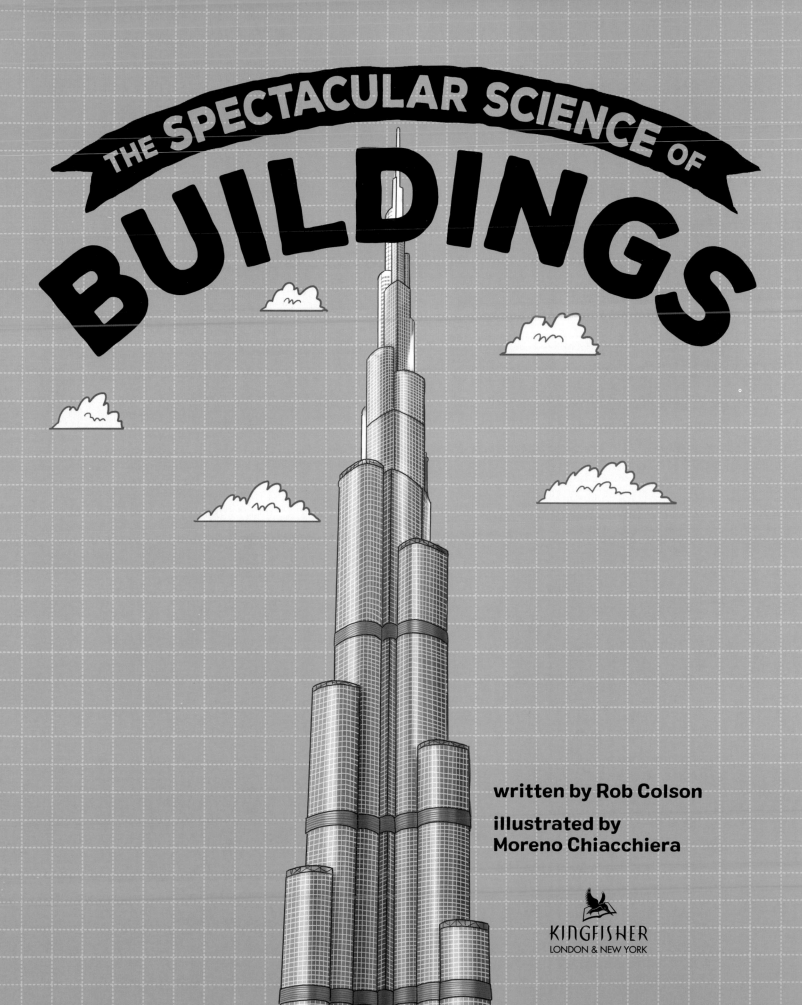

written by Rob Colson

illustrated by
Moreno Chiacchiera

KINGFISHER
LONDON & NEW YORK

KINGFISHER
LONDON & NEW YORK

First published 2023 in the United States
by Kingfisher
120 Broadway, New York, NY 10271
Kingfisher is an imprint of
Macmillan Children's Books, London
All rights reserved.

Copyright © Macmillan Publishers
International Ltd 2023

ISBN 978-0-7534-7904-9

Distributed in the U.S. and Canada by Macmillan,
120 Broadway, New York, NY 10271

Library of Congress Cataloging-in-Publication
data has been applied for.

Author: Rob Colson
Illustrator: Moreno Chiacchiera
Consultant: Penny Johnson
Designed and edited by Tall Tree Ltd

Kingfisher Books are available for special
promotions and premiums.
For details contact:
Special Markets Department, Macmillan
120 Broadway, New York, NY 10271.

For more information please visit:
www.kingfisherbooks.com

Printed in China
2 4 6 8 9 7 5 3 1
1TR/0323/WKT/RV/128MA

EU representative:
1st Floor, The Liffey Trust Centre
117-126 Sheriff Street Upper,
Dublin 1 D01 YC43

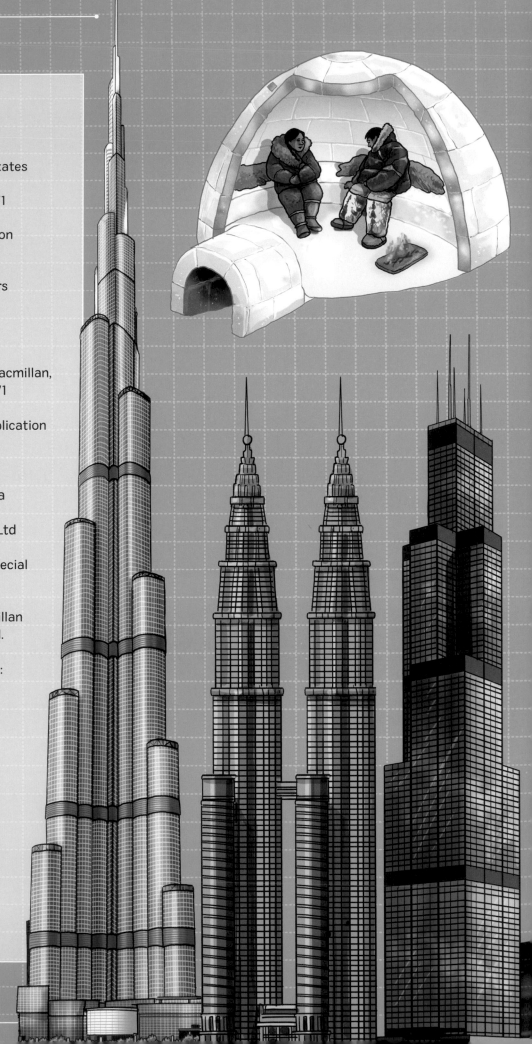

CONTENTS

WHERE IT STARTED

Nobody knows when the first permanent buildings were made, but it is likely that they were built around 10,000 BCE when people first settled in towns and cities. Today, we use the latest scientific knowledge to make buildings that are bigger, stronger, and safer than ever before.

THE FIRST CITIES

The first large cities were built in a region called Mesopotamia in modern-day Iraq. One of the most important of these early settlements was the Sumerian city of Ur, which grew big and powerful around 3800 BCE. Three well-preserved buildings remain from ancient Ur, including the Great Ziggurat. Ziggurats were huge temples built of mud bricks.

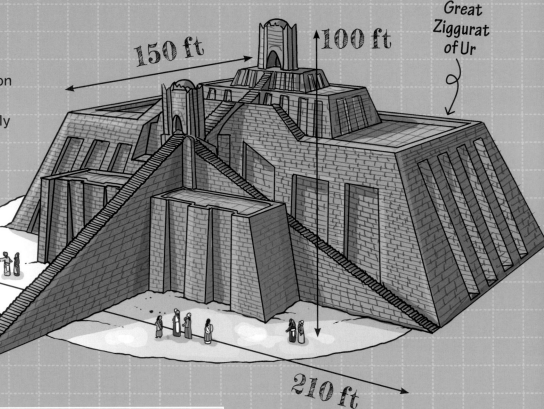

150 ft

100 ft

Great Ziggurat of Ur

210 ft

ZAHA HADID

British-Iraqi architect Zaha Hadid (1950–2016) was inspired by childhood visits to ancient ruins in Iraq. Her designs include museums, opera houses, sports stadiums, and airports around the world. Hadid created eye-catching buildings that combined sharp angles with sweeping curves.

Heydar Aliyev Centre, in Baku, Azerbaijan

GÖBEKLI TEPE

The oldest permanent settlement ever discovered is called Göbekli Tepe in Turkey. The town was built around 9000 BCE, soon after the end of the last Ice Age. The remains of the Göbekli Tepe were discovered by archaeologists in 1996.

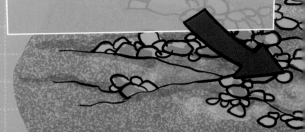

SCIENCE IN DESIGN

Architects and civil engineers test out their structures by placing models in wind tunnels to study the effects of strong winds. They also use computer simulations to test their designs.

ARCHITECTS

Architects design all kinds of buildings. Like civil engineers, architects need to make sure that their buildings are strong and safe, but they also create spaces that are good for people to live or work in. Architects sometimes have fun with their buildings, designing something that is spectacular to look at.

CIVIL ENGINEERS

Civil engineers design and oversee the construction of large structures such as buildings, bridges, tunnels, roads, and dams. For a civil engineer, the main concern is to ensure that the structure is strong and safe. To do this, they need to understand many aspects of science, including the properties of materials and the strengths and weaknesses of different shapes.

THE PYRAMIDS OF GIZA

The Pyramids of Giza in Cairo, Egypt, are a group of huge limestone pyramids that were built more than 4,500 years ago. The largest pyramid, the Great Pyramid, was the tallest building in the world for nearly 4,000 years.

ROYAL TOMBS

Constructed over a period of about 25 years between 2550 BCE and 2520 BCE, the Great Pyramid of Giza was built as a tomb for the pharaoh Khufu. The Pyramid of Khafre was built as a tomb for Khufu's son Khafre. It appears larger, but this is because it stands on higher ground. The smaller Pyramid of Menkaure was completed a few decades later.

440

200 ft

GLEAMING WHITE

When they were completed, the pyramids were covered in a layer of gleaming white limestone. The polished surfaces would have glistened in the sunlight. Over the years, these outer layers were removed and used to construct other buildings.

Pyramid of Menkaure

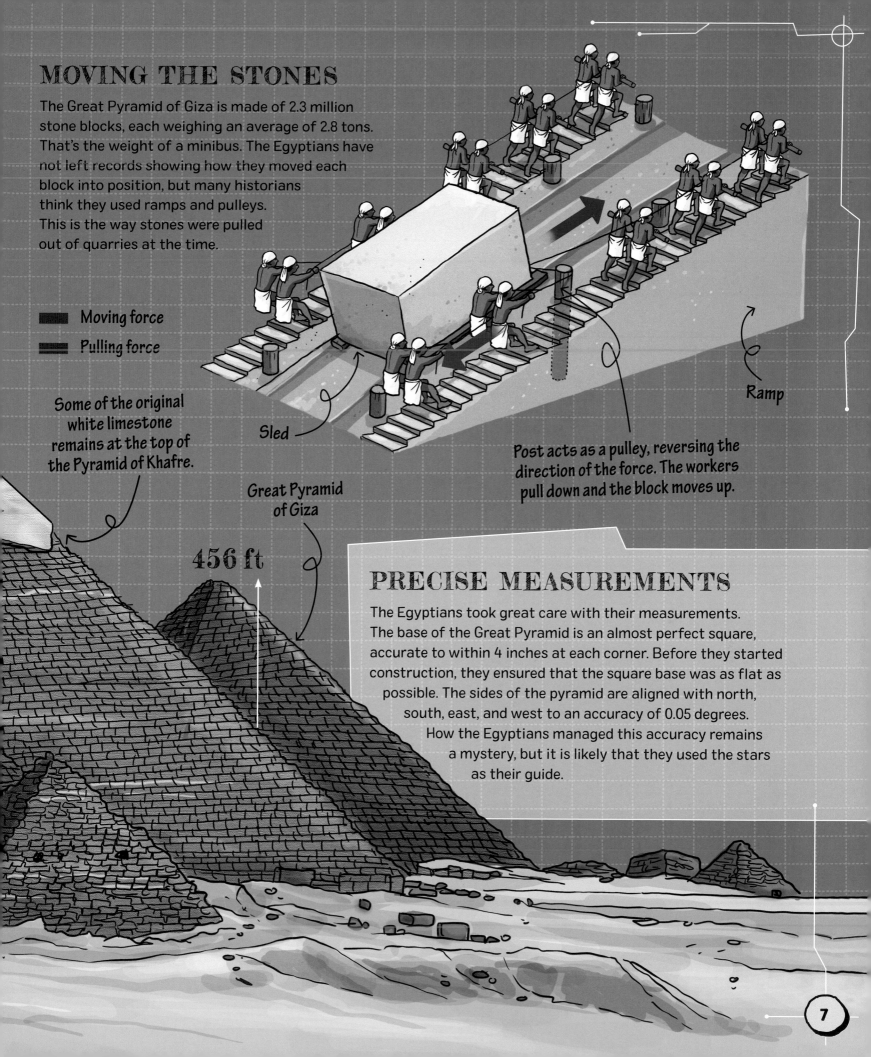

MOVING THE STONES

The Great Pyramid of Giza is made of 2.3 million stone blocks, each weighing an average of 2.8 tons. That's the weight of a minibus. The Egyptians have not left records showing how they moved each block into position, but many historians think they used ramps and pulleys. This is the way stones were pulled out of quarries at the time.

█ Moving force

█ Pulling force

Ramp

Sled

Post acts as a pulley, reversing the direction of the force. The workers pull down and the block moves up.

Some of the original white limestone remains at the top of the Pyramid of Khafre.

Great Pyramid of Giza

456 ft

PRECISE MEASUREMENTS

The Egyptians took great care with their measurements. The base of the Great Pyramid is an almost perfect square, accurate to within 4 inches at each corner. Before they started construction, they ensured that the square base was as flat as possible. The sides of the pyramid are aligned with north, south, east, and west to an accuracy of 0.05 degrees. How the Egyptians managed this accuracy remains a mystery, but it is likely that they used the stars as their guide.

ANCIENT GREEK ARCHITECTURE

The Ancient Greeks created buildings with enormous attention to detail, using pleasing proportions and shapes. They are best-known for building impressive stone temples. The most famous of these temples, the Parthenon, is still standing on the Acropolis in Athens.

OPTICAL ILLUSION

The Parthenon is a 2,500-year-old temple that sits on a rocky outcrop above the city of Athens. The building was carefully designed to give the illusion of straight lines and right angles when viewed from a distance of about 200 feet down the slope. But a closer look reveals that this is a clever optical illusion.

Parthenon

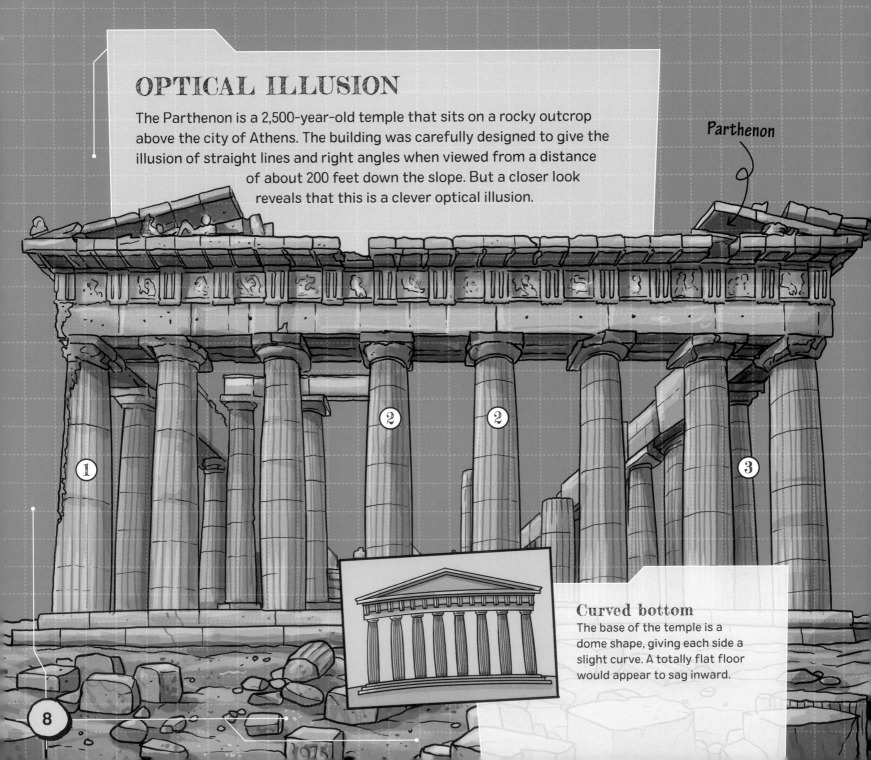

Curved bottom
The base of the temple is a dome shape, giving each side a slight curve. A totally flat floor would appear to sag inward.

CRAZY COLUMNS

1. The columns lean very slightly inward. If they were extended upward, the columns would all meet at a point 7,875 feet high. This makes the columns appear vertical when viewed from below. If they were actually vertical, they would appear to be toppling over.

2. The columns swell slightly in the middle. If they were completely straight, they would look like they were narrower in the middle.

3. The columns at the ends are wider and more spaced out than the columns in the center. Viewed from a distance, the spacing appears equal.

A PERFECT THEATER

The Greeks built semicircular outdoor amphitheaters to perform plays and concerts. The greatest of these was the Theater of Epidaurus, which was famed for the quality of its sound. In 2007, scientists discovered that the secret of the theater's incredible acoustics lay in its rows of limestone seats. The stone absorbs low-frequency background noises while reflecting the high-frequency sounds coming from the stage, allowing the actors' voices to reach all the way to the back row.

The chorus performed in the circular area in front of the stage.

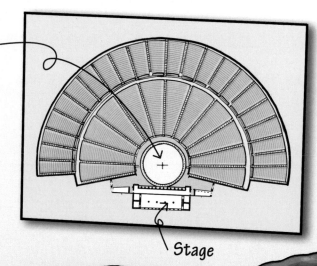

Stage

The Theater of Epidaurus could hold 13,000 people.

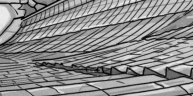

GREAT WALL OF CHINA

The Great Wall of China is one of the largest building projects ever undertaken. In fact, it is not just one wall but a series of walls built across the frontier of northern China to keep out invaders from Mongolia. The first sections were erected nearly 3,000 years ago and construction continued for more than 2,000 years.

MING DYNASTY SECTIONS

The best-preserved section of the wall was built during the Ming dynasty (1368–1644). This section is 5,500 miles long (shown in red on the map, right).

The total length of all sections of the wall is more than **13,000 miles.** That's more than half the circumference of Earth.

■ Ming dynasty section

■ Older sections

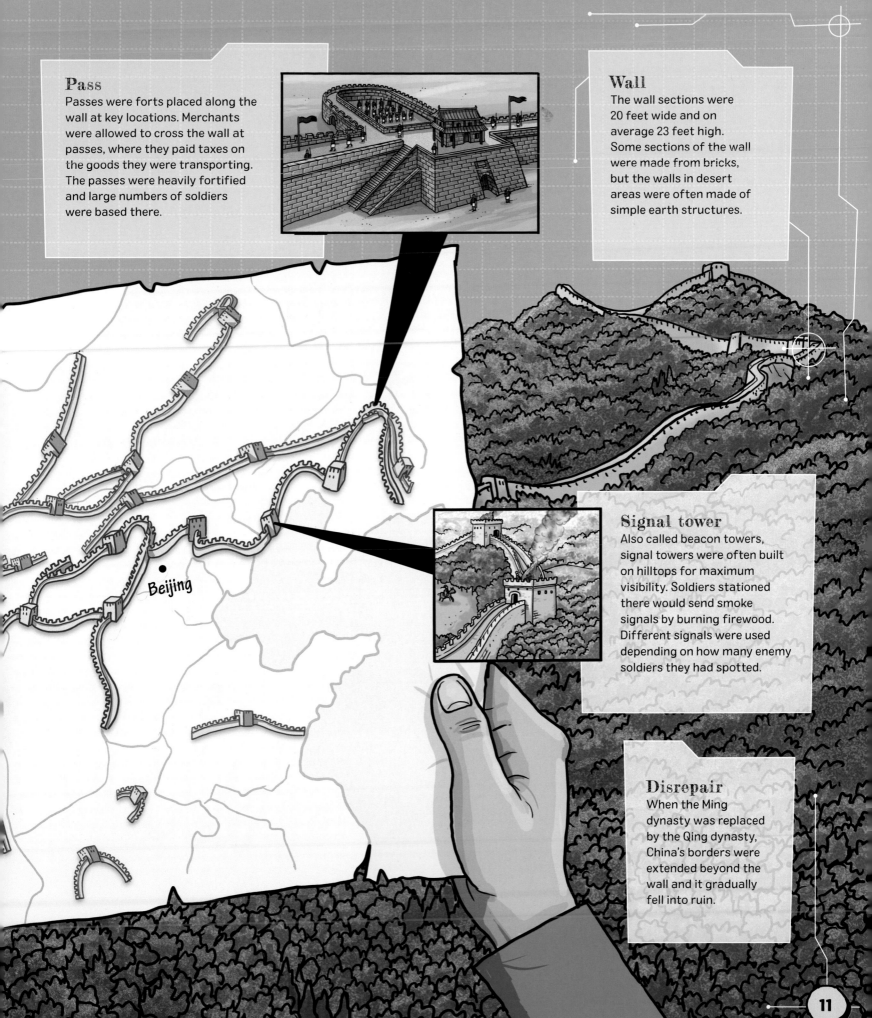

Pass
Passes were forts placed along the wall at key locations. Merchants were allowed to cross the wall at passes, where they paid taxes on the goods they were transporting. The passes were heavily fortified and large numbers of soldiers were based there.

Wall
The wall sections were 20 feet wide and on average 23 feet high. Some sections of the wall were made from bricks, but the walls in desert areas were often made of simple earth structures.

Beijing

Signal tower
Also called beacon towers, signal towers were often built on hilltops for maximum visibility. Soldiers stationed there would send smoke signals by burning firewood. Different signals were used depending on how many enemy soldiers they had spotted.

Disrepair
When the Ming dynasty was replaced by the Qing dynasty, China's borders were extended beyond the wall and it gradually fell into ruin.

SAGRADA FAMILIA

The Sagrada Familia is a large cathedral in Barcelona, Spain. Its construction began in 1882, and 140 years later, it is still not finished. Generations of architects have worked on the building following the plans of the original architect, Antoni Gaudí.

ROBOT STONE MASONS

The pace of construction has increased in recent years due to the use of modern technology. While all the stone was once carved by hand, today computer-controlled robotic carving machines cut the stones into exactly the right shapes.

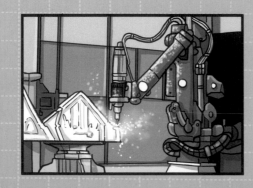

FAMILY OF SPIRES

Gaudí designed a building with 18 spires, each one representing a different figure from Christianity. Together, they would form the Sagrada Familia, which means "sacred family" in Spanish. By 2021, just nine of these spires had been completed, and construction work is likely to continue for some time yet. When it is finished, the large central spire is planned to be 566 feet high, which will make the Sagrada Familia the tallest Christian church in the world.

ANTONI GAUDÍ

There are 14 buildings designed by architect Antoni Gaudí (1852–1926) dotted around Barcelona, the city in which he spent his whole working life. His designs helped to create a new style of architecture known as Catalan Art Nouveau. Their distinctive forms were inspired by nature, using curved shapes drawn from plants and flowers. Gaudí worked on the Sagrada Familia for more than 40 years, knowing that it would not be completed in his lifetime.

Antoni Gaudí

A multicoloured salamander designed by Gaudí stands at the entrance to Park Güell in Barcelona. It is popularly known as "The Dragon."

EIFFEL TOWER

The Eiffel Tower in Paris is a building made entirely of iron girders. Built for the World Exhibition in 1889, it stands 1,083 feet high and was the world's tallest structure for 40 years.

NEW KIND OF TOWER

The organizers of the World Exhibition chose the design of bridge engineer Gustave Eiffel over more than 100 other proposals. Some people doubted that a structure so tall made only of iron could stand up, but Eiffel used his knowledge of metalwork to create a structure that was lightweight but very strong. It was completed in two years, ready to serve as the entrance to the exhibition.

BUILDING WITH TRIANGLES

There are 186 triangles in the Eiffel Tower. Eiffel knew from his experience building railway bridges that triangles are an extremely strong shape to build with. The weight pressing down on the top corner of a triangle is distributed evenly down each side. The two girders on the side of the triangle are squeezed, or compressed, while the bottom girder is pulled, or under tension.

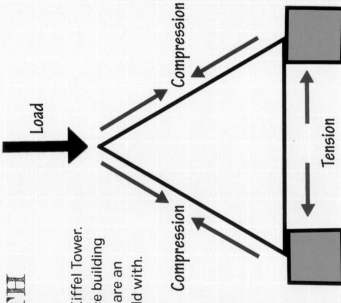

Load

Compression

Compression

Tension

Antenna
A television antenna was added in 1957, increasing its height by 62 feet. A new antenna was installed in 2022, adding a further 30 feet.

The top observation platform is **906 feet high.**

Stopping the rust
The tower is completely repainted every seven years to stop it from rusting. Sixty tons of paint is used.

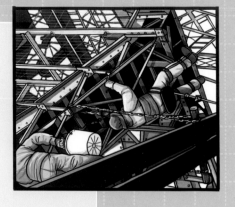

GUSTAVE EIFFEL

Alexandre–Gustav Eiffel (1832–1923) was a French civil engineer who specialized in designing strong metal structures such as railway bridges. Before designing the tower that bears his name, Eiffel created a metal framework for the Statue of Liberty, a monument in New York Harbor that was a gift to the USA from France.

Curving in
The tower stands on four piers, which curve inwards to form a single central column. The glass elevators ascend in a curve up the piers.

SKYSCRAPERS

In the 1880s, a new kind of building appeared in cities around the USA. These were the first skyscrapers—buildings more than 10 stories high. Within a few decades, skyscrapers had transformed the skylines of cities around the world.

TECHNOLOGICAL ADVANCES

A number of technological developments encouraged the building of skyscrapers in the 1880s.

1. In 1855, English inventor Henry Bessemer (1813–1898) developed a new process to mass-produce steel. This made it cheaper to construct tall buildings around steel skeletons, which would bear most of their weight. Built in 1889, the 13-story Tacoma Building in Chicago was the first skyscraper with "curtain walls" on the outside. These are walls that do not bear the building's weight.

Tacoma Building

2. In 1879, American Thomas Edison (1847–1931) invented the electric light bulb. Electric lighting allowed the large spaces inside skyscrapers to be lit much more easily.

3. New designs for electric elevators were developed in the early 1880s. Safe, reliable, and fast elevators were needed to carry people to the higher floors.

Willis Tower, Chicago (1974) 1,450 feet

Empire State Building, New York (1931) 1,250 feet

Singer Building, New York (1898) 673 feet

Home Insurance Building, Chicago (1885) 180 feet

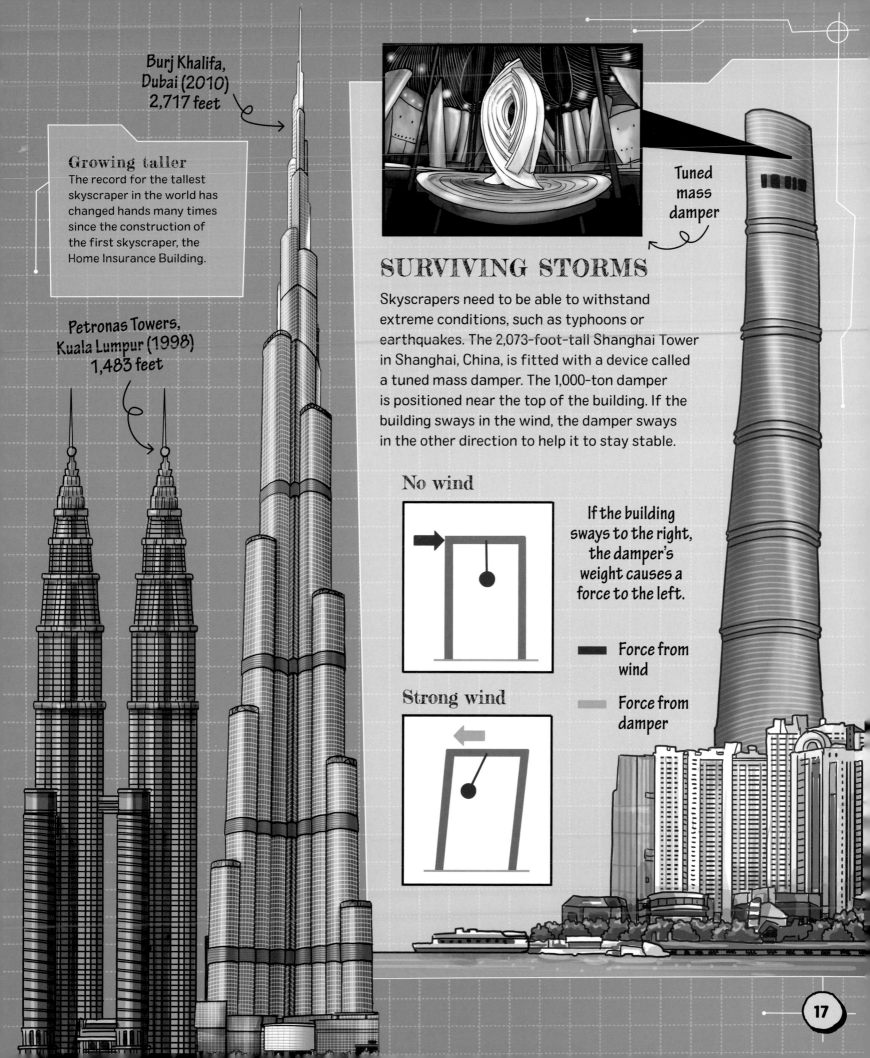

Burj Khalifa,
Dubai (2010)
2,717 feet

Growing taller
The record for the tallest skyscraper in the world has changed hands many times since the construction of the first skyscraper, the Home Insurance Building.

Petronas Towers,
Kuala Lumpur (1998)
1,483 feet

Tuned
mass
damper

SURVIVING STORMS

Skyscrapers need to be able to withstand extreme conditions, such as typhoons or earthquakes. The 2,073-foot-tall Shanghai Tower in Shanghai, China, is fitted with a device called a tuned mass damper. The 1,000-ton damper is positioned near the top of the building. If the building sways in the wind, the damper sways in the other direction to help it to stay stable.

No wind

If the building sways to the right, the damper's weight causes a force to the left.

Strong wind

━━ Force from wind

━━ Force from damper

BURJ KHALIFA

Standing 2,717 feet high, the Burj Khalifa in Dubai is the tallest building in the world. Sometimes described as a "vertical city," the skyscraper contains a number of hotels, restaurants and shops. It is also home to more than 1,000 permanent residents.

732-foot spire

sits on the top of the building. It contains communications antennas. Only maintenance staff are allowed into the spire.

The building contains

57 elevators,

which travel at speeds of 30 feet per second. You could also reach the highest inhabited floor, Level 160, by climbing 2,909 stairs. To climb any higher, you need a ladder.

Outdoor deck

On the 124th floor, at a height of 1,483 feet, is an outdoor observation deck. On a clear day it is possible to see across to Iran, 95 miles away, but don't look down!

STRUCTURAL SYSTEM

The spiraling Y-shaped design is inspired by the Hymenocallis flower. Each tier of the building steps back in a spiral pattern up the building, which helps to deflect wind around the structure. This stops the wind from forming whirlpools of air currents, which would damage the building.

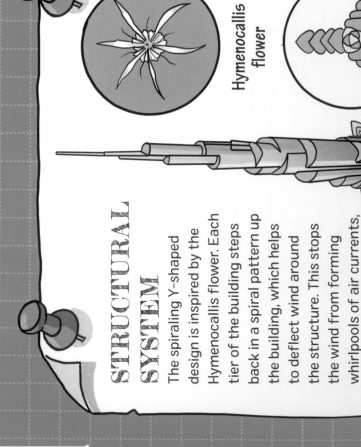

Hymenocallis flower

Spiral design

One of the world's highest swimming pools is located on Level 76 at a height of

886 feet.

After every 30 floors,

several stories (or floors) are used for machinery to run the building. These contain electricity substations, water tanks, and air conditioning units.

Keeping cool

In the fierce desert heat, keeping buildings cool is a big challenge. The Burj Khalifa solves this problem by creating a massive reservoir of ice. The cooling system makes ice at night. It uses the ice during the heat of the day to cool the building. Water chilled by the ice to 37°F is pumped around the building.

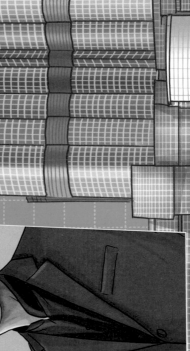

In the clouds

It takes a team of 120 window cleaners three months to clean the entire building. There are a whopping 24,348 windows, and the cleaners start from the top and work down.

900 residential

apartments are situated between floors 19 and 108.

ADRIAN SMITH

The Burj Khalifa was designed by the US architect Adrian Smith (born 1944), who specializes in building super-tall skyscrapers. Smith also designed the unfinished Jeddah Tower in Jeddah, Saudi Arabia. Work on the tower was paused in 2018. If construction is completed according to Smith's design, it will become the first building in history to stand 1 kilometer (3,281 feet) high.

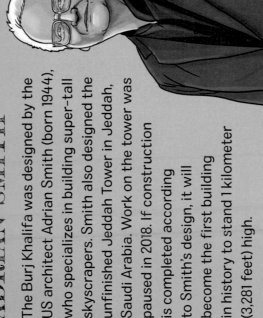

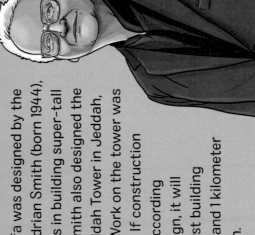

BUILDING WITH MUD

Measuring 330 feet long and 130 feet wide, the Great Mosque of Djenné in Mali is the largest mud building in the world. Its imposing pillars dominate the skyline of the small town of Djenné.

MUD AND PLASTER

A mosque was first built on the site in Djenné about 800 years ago. The current building was built on the ruins of the old building and dates back to 1907. It is made from sun-baked mud and straw bricks. The bricks are covered in plaster made from a material called banco, which is a mix of clay, rice bran, shea butter, baobab powder, and water.

At the tip of each pillar is placed an ostrich egg, a traditional symbol of fertility. Bundles of palm sticks, known as toron, stick out from the walls. The toron act as a ready-made scaffolding for men to stand on during the annual replastering.

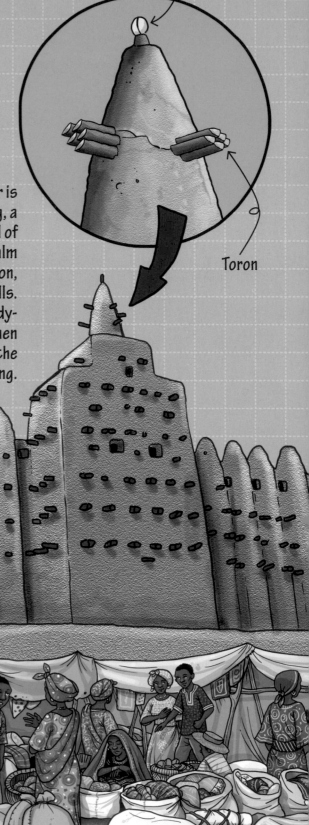

Ostrich egg

Toron

The mosque overlooks the central market of Djenné.

PLASTERING THE WALLS

Every April, the people of Djenné come together for a one-day event called the Crépissage (Plastering). Supervised by professional masons, teams of young men scramble up the walls to cover them with new layers of banco. The Crépissage starts at 4 am and they are all finished by 9 am, just as the sun starts to bake the building once again. The new plaster protects the mosque from the heavy rains that fall in July and August.

52 ft

Keeping cool

The mosque's design keeps it cool inside even in the hot summer months, when the temperature outside soars over 100°F. The mud walls insulate the building from the heat, while holes in the roof covered with terracotta lids allow fresh air to circulate freely.

COMPUTER MODEL

The Zamani Project, a research group based in Cape Town, South Africa, has produced an accurate 3D computer model of the Great Mosque of Djenné. They scanned the building with lasers to measure every part of it in minute detail. If you go online, you can see the results for yourself. The Zamani Project has produced models of ancient buildings all over Africa, providing an accurate record to help conserve them for the future.

BUILDING WITH WOOD

More than two-thirds of Sweden is covered in forests, and Swedes have developed new ways to create buildings using wood. The Sara Cultural Centre and Wood Hotel in the northern town of Skellefteå, just below the Arctic Circle, is the world's first wooden skyscraper, built entirely from local trees.

246 ft

20 stories high, 246 feet tall, the Wood Hotel sits on top of the Cultural Centre.

At the bottom of the building, the Sara Cultural Centre features two theaters and a museum.

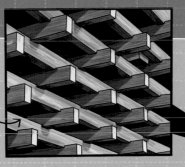

Glulam

STRONG LAYERS

The columns and beams that support the auditoriums for the theaters are made from glulam, a material made from parallel layers of timber that have been glued together. The walls and floors are made from cross-laminated timber (CLT), made from layers of timber laid at right-angles to each other. CLT is strong in all directions. The structure is light but very strong. To stop it from swaying too much in the wind, concrete was used for the top two floors to add weight.

The main auditorium seats 1,200 people.

Cheap and clean

The room pods for the hotel were manufactured in factories and slotted into place ready-made. This made the construction process very swift, with a whole story of the hotel completed every two days. The architects hope that the building will inspire similar projects around the world, resulting in many more so-called "plyscrapers" in the towns and cities of the future.

ECO-TOWN

Building with wood forms part of a wider plan to make Skellefteå an eco-friendly place to live. The town runs entirely on renewable energy, producing its electricity from hydropower (running water), wind turbines, and biofuels (fuels made from plants or food waste). The excess heat produced by the biofuel power plant (pictured below) is fed back into the system to heat people's homes. The town also maintains a shared pool of electric cars so that everyone can drive using renewable energy.

BUILDING WITH ICE

The Inuit of North America have made temporary homes out of snow for thousands of years. A unique hotel in Sweden now does the same thing with ice.

SLEEPING ON ICE

The Icehotel in northern Sweden was first built in 1989. It gives its guests the opportunity to sleep in a building made entirely from ice! The rooms are kept at a chilly temperature of 23°F. Guests sleep in special thermal sleeping bags on top of an ice bed covered in reindeer skins.

The Icehotel melts in spring and has to be rebuilt each November. It is made from blocks of ice carved from the frozen surface of the nearby Torne River.

Each year, artists are invited to create spectacular ice sculptures for the hotel. Like the rest of the structure, the sculptures melt away in the spring.

IGLOOS

Igloos are buildings made from bricks of compacted snow. While the snow itself is freezing cold, an igloo can keep you at a comfortable 60°F, even when the temperature outside plunges. The bricks may look solid, but most of the space is occupied by air trapped between tiny crystals. These miniature air pockets provide excellent insulation from the cold outside.

Small air vents in the roof allow smoke from the fire to escape.

Sleeping quarters are raised to where the air is warmer as the cold air sinks to the bottom.

The entrance is located at the bottom. You enter through a tunnel, which prevents chilly winds from blowing into the igloo.

GOLDEN GATE BRIDGE

Spanning a treacherous strait at the entrance to San Francisco Bay in California, the 1.7-mile-long Golden Gate Bridge was the longest suspension bridge in the world when it was opened in 1937.

HOW IT WORKS

A suspension bridge supports the weight of the roadway with cables strung over large towers. The cables are secured at either end of the bridge by blocks called anchorages. Some parts of the bridge are being pulled, or under tension, while other parts of the bridge are being squashed, or under compression.

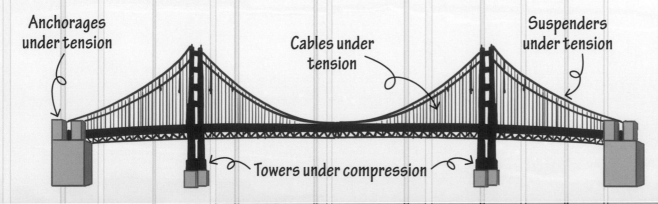

Anchorages under tension

Cables under tension

Suspenders under tension

Towers under compression

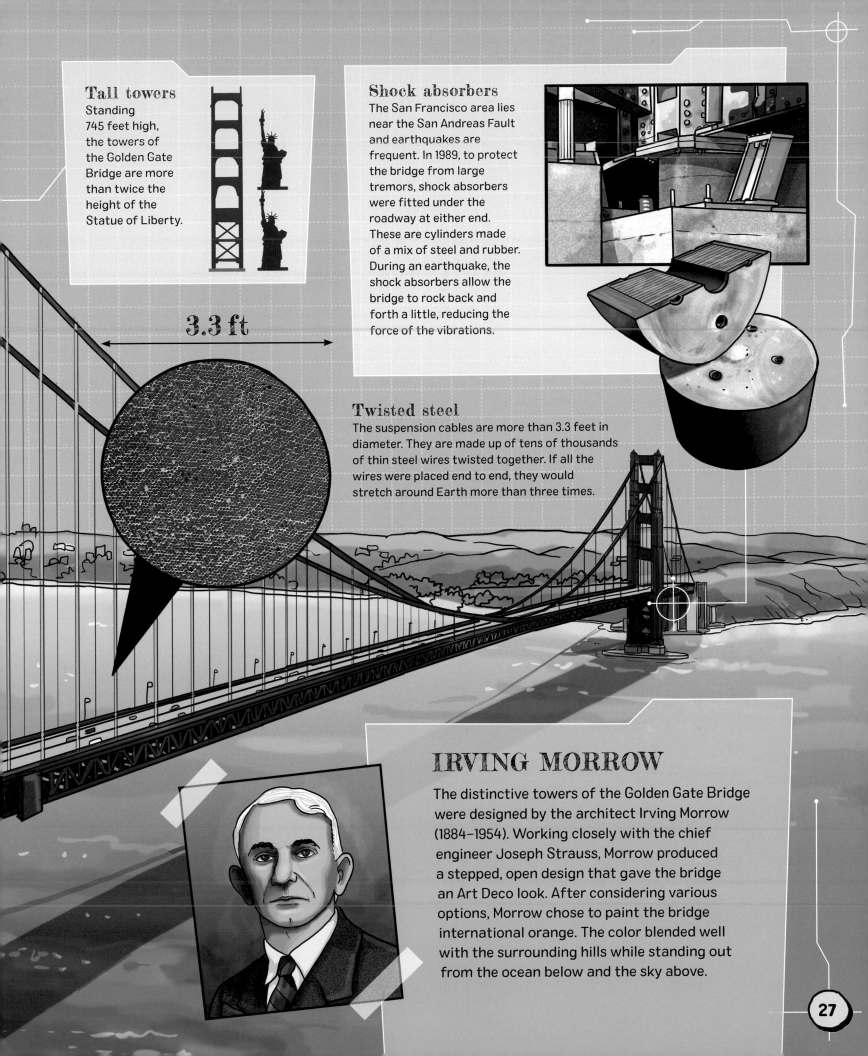

Tall towers

Standing 745 feet high, the towers of the Golden Gate Bridge are more than twice the height of the Statue of Liberty.

Shock absorbers

The San Francisco area lies near the San Andreas Fault and earthquakes are frequent. In 1989, to protect the bridge from large tremors, shock absorbers were fitted under the roadway at either end. These are cylinders made of a mix of steel and rubber. During an earthquake, the shock absorbers allow the bridge to rock back and forth a little, reducing the force of the vibrations.

3.3 ft

Twisted steel

The suspension cables are more than 3.3 feet in diameter. They are made up of tens of thousands of thin steel wires twisted together. If all the wires were placed end to end, they would stretch around Earth more than three times.

IRVING MORROW

The distinctive towers of the Golden Gate Bridge were designed by the architect Irving Morrow (1884–1954). Working closely with the chief engineer Joseph Strauss, Morrow produced a stepped, open design that gave the bridge an Art Deco look. After considering various options, Morrow chose to paint the bridge international orange. The color blended well with the surrounding hills while standing out from the ocean below and the sky above.

MILLAU VIADUCT

The Millau Viaduct is a road bridge that spans the Tarn Valley in southern France. At a height of 1,102 feet, it is the tallest bridge in the world.

The masts are **285 feet high.**

Pier 2 is the tallest pier, standing **804 feet high.**

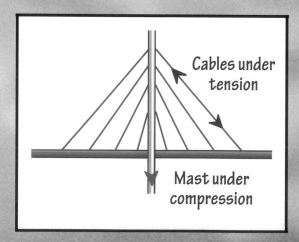

Cables under tension

Mast under compression

CABLE-STAYED BRIDGE

The Millau Viaduct is a cable-stayed bridge. The road deck is held up by cables that fan out on either side of seven masts. The cables are stretched, or under tension, while the masts are squeezed, or compressed.

CURVING SHAPE

The 1.6-mile-long bridge curves as part of the circumference of a circle with a radius of 12 miles. The curve was added to give road users a better view of their surroundings. A straight bridge would have made it seem to drivers as if they were floating in the air.

154 cable stays

hold up the deck. They are made of intertwined strands of steel.

To improve visibility for drivers, the deck is inclined at a

3°angle.

SPEEDY CONSTRUCTION

Construction of the bridge went very smoothly. It began in 2001 with the building of the seven piers on which the bridge stands. These were completed in 2003. The steel decks were made separately in 18 sections. The sections were pushed out over the piers using hydraulic lifting machines.

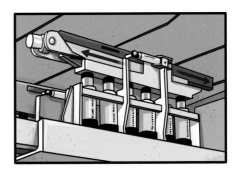

A hydraulic machine underneath each deck slowly slid it into place.

Once the decks were in place, the masts were constructed and the cables fixed in place. Finally, the road surface was laid. The first cars crossed the bridge on December 16, 2004.

CHANNEL TUNNEL

Completed in 1994, the Channel Tunnel passes underneath the English Channel to link Britain with France. It has the longest underwater section of any tunnel in the world, measuring 23.5 miles.

FULFILLING A DREAM

The first plan for a Channel Tunnel (left) was drawn up in 1802 by French engineer Albert Mathieu-Favier, who imagined a tunnel for horse-drawn carriages with an artificial island halfway along to allow a change of horses. Over the next century, extensive railway networks were built and new plans imagined a tunnel for trains. France and the UK finally agreed to build a tunnel in 1964, but it took another 22 years to put the plans and finances in place to finally start.

CHOOSING THE ROUTE

The path of the tunnel follows a layer of rock called marly chalk, which was the safest rock for the tunnel to run through. In order to stay in this layer, the tunnel reached its deepest point 360 feet below sea level and under 246 feet of rock. Tunnellers worked from both the British side and the French side. They started on the same day in 1988 and met in the middle three years later.

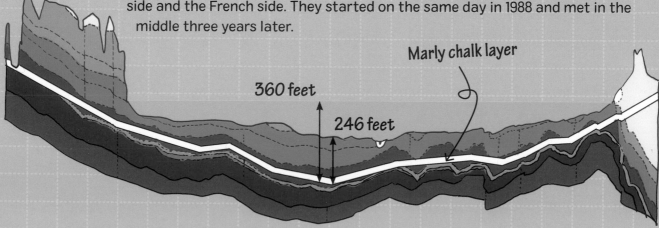

Marly chalk layer

360 feet

246 feet

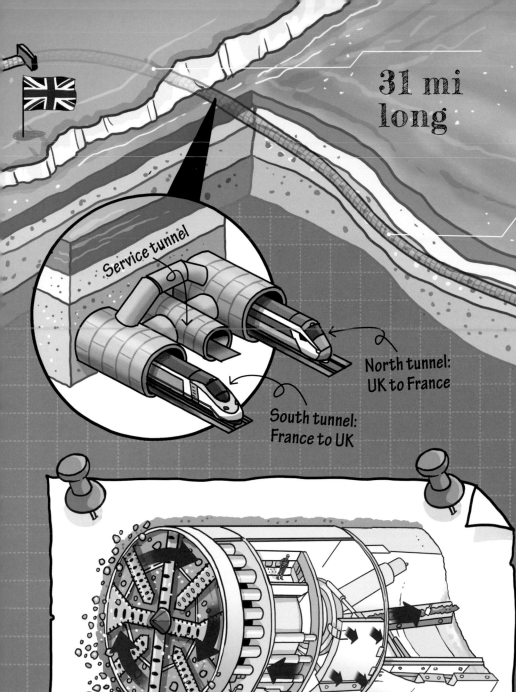

31 mi long

23.5 mi undersea section

Service tunnel

North tunnel: UK to France

South tunnel: France to UK

Service tunnel
There are two separate tunnels for trains, connected by a central service tunnel, which is kept at a higher air pressure to prevent smoke or fumes from entering.

TUNNEL BORING MACHINES

Eleven specially built tunnel boring machines (TBMs) were used to cut through the rock. Each TBM was 26.5 feet wide and more than 650 feet long. The spinning blades at the front of the TBMs advanced at a speed of about 15 feet per hour. The rock was transported to the surface by conveyor belts. On the English side, the rock was used to create an artificial landmass called Samphire Hoe, which is now a nature reserve.

Train service
Both high-speed passenger trains and freight trains use the tunnel. More than 20 million passengers, 2.5 million cars, and 1.5 million trucks are carried through the tunnel each year. The trains travel at a maximum speed of 100 mph, and it takes them 20 minutes to pass through the tunnel.

ANGKOR WAT

Standing at the edge of the ancient city of Angkor in Cambodia, Angkor Wat is the largest religious building in the world. Built entirely of stone, the temple is covered in beautiful carvings depicting scenes from Hindu mythology.

EPIC PROJECT

Construction of the temple began in the year 1116 CE under the reign of the Khmer King Suryavarman II. It was completed just 30 years later, shortly after the king's death. It was built of nearly 10 million sandstone blocks, many weighing more than 1 ton each. A team of more than 300,000 people was needed to complete the work, including architects, builders, stone masons, and sculptors.

Mythical mountains
The five central towers of Angkor Wat represent the summits of the mythical Mount Meru, which is said to be the home of the gods in Hindu mythology. The temple complex is ringed by a 13-foot-deep moat, which represents the ocean said to surround Mount Meru. The moat also helps to stabilize the temple's foundations, keeping the amount of water in the ground at a regular level.

The Sun rises directly above the central tower each equinox.

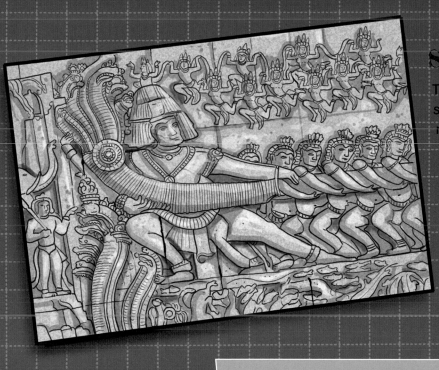

STONE CARVINGS

The detailed carvings were made directly into the stone on-site, meaning that the sculptors had no room for error. The carvings are known as bas-reliefs, meaning that the sculpted figures project just a little from the stone surface behind them. Each individual person depicted has unique features. In total, there are 13,000 square feet of bas relief carvings on Angkor Wat. These include an illustration of *The Churning of the Ocean of Milk*, a story about the creation of the universe, in which good wins over evil.

RESTORING THE TOWERS

In 2022, a year-long project to restore the central Bakan tower was completed. Centuries of rainwater had eroded the tower's laterite foundation stones. Laterite is a rock that contains high levels of iron oxide, which gives it a distinctive red color. A team of stonemasons replaced the damaged stones, some of which weighed more than 3 tons. The team also returned stones scattered around the base of the tower back to their original places to help support the pillars. Restoration work on Angkor Wat will continue into the future to ensure that the temple does not collapse.

SYDNEY OPERA HOUSE

Sydney Opera House, sitting on the banks of Sydney Harbour, is one of the most famous buildings in the world. The construction process was plagued with problems and the project ran over time and budget, but the end result was a spectacular building that has become a national symbol of Australia.

Jørn Utzon

Danish architect Jørn Utzon (1918–2008) beat more than 200 other architects in a competition to design the Sydney Opera House. Utzon stated that he came up with the design for the roof while peeling an orange, imagining that the shells of the roof would all be parts of a sphere. Due to delays and rising costs, Utzon left the project in 1966, and he was not invited to the opening ceremony in 1973. However, in later life his extraordinary achievement was widely recognized and the Opera House was made a World Heritage Site the year before he died.

CASTING THE ROOF

The roof is made up of a series of gleaming white concrete shells, designed to resemble the sails of a ship. It took a team of architects and engineers six years to work out how to build the roof. Eventually they hit upon the solution: each shell was made as a section taken from a sphere. This allowed the team to cast arches of different lengths from the same mould. In total, the roof is made of 4,000 panels and 2,400 supporting ribs. The team used computers to work out how to assemble the arches in a way that gave maximum strength. This was one of the first times computers had been used in architecture.

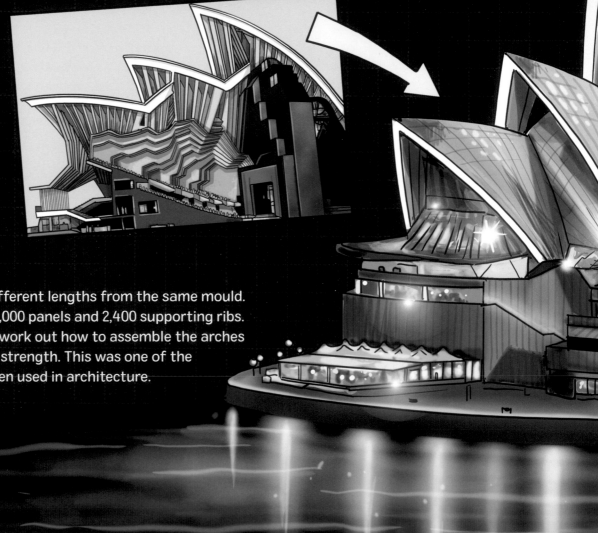

IMPROVING THE SOUND

While audiences marvelled at the Concert Hall's amazing design, they criticized its acoustics. Sounds bounced unevenly off the high ceiling, and the sound quality varied depending on where you were sitting. To solve this problem, in 2016 18 petal-shaped wooden reflectors were suspended from the ceiling above the stage. The reflectors bounced sounds towards the audience, ensuring that everyone heard all the sounds clearly.

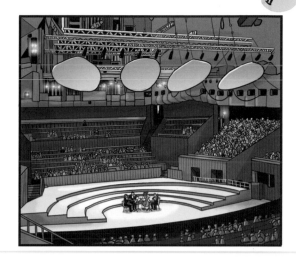

KEEPING COOL

The Opera House's air conditioning system takes seawater from Sydney Harbour to provide cool air. Water flows through 22 miles of pipes to keep each part of the building at just the right temperature. On-stage, the temperature during performances must be kept at 72.5°F to ensure that the orchestra's musical instruments stay in tune.

THREE GORGES DAM

Fully operational since 2012, the Three Gorges Dam across the Yangtze River in China is the world's largest power station.

TYPES OF DAM

Dams hold back the force of water in various ways. Many dams use a combination of these ways. For instance, a dam may be both an arch dam and a buttress dam.

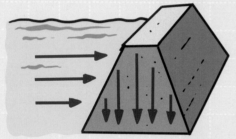

Gravity dam
The force of the water is directed downward.

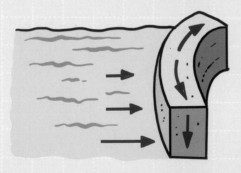

Arch dam
The force of the water is directed outward into the rock on either side of the dam.

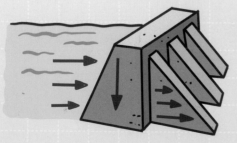

Buttress dam
The force of the water is directed downward and through a series of buttresses, or supports.

Heavyweight
The Three Gorges Dam is a gravity dam. It is made from a mix of concrete and steel and weighs 44 million tons. That's seven times the weight of the Great Pyramid of Giza. It is 594 feet high and 7,660 feet long.

7,660 feet

FLOODING THE VALLEY

The building of the dam created a long, thin lake called the Three Gorges Reservoir. The reservoir extends 370 miles behind the dam, with an average width of 3,300 feet. The reservoir flooded entire towns, and more than 1 million people had to leave their homes upstream of the dam. Cities located downstream of the dam are now protected from seasonal floods as the amount of water passing through the dam can be controlled.

Jialing River

Reservoir

Sandouping

Dam

Chongqing

Yangzi River

GENERATING ELECTRICITY

The dam produces 100 TWh (terawatt-hours) of electricity each year. That's roughly equivalent to the energy use of the city of Beijing, which has a population of 21 million people. It does this by passing water under high pressure through 32 separate turbines. The water makes the turbines spin, and a generator turns this energy into electricity.

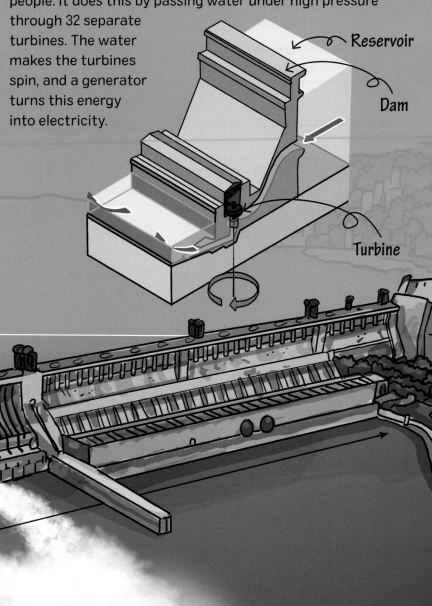

Reservoir

Dam

Turbine

PETRONIUS OIL PLATFORM

The Petronius Platform in the Gulf of Mexico is the tallest offshore oil rig in the world, but most of this massive structure is hidden under water.

Dangerous job

Drilling for oil and gas never stops, and the work is dangerous and noisy. Workers live on the platform for two weeks at a time, operating in shifts to keep the oil flowing day and night.

The legs are flexible, allowing the platform to sway from side to side in the ocean currents. It can move by up to

26 feet.

Empire State Building

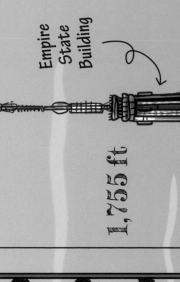

1,755 ft

The top of the platform is several stories high. It contains the drilling rig, processing equipment, and living quarters.

Oil and gas

The Petronius rig extracts 280,000 ft³ of oil every day. That's enough to fill the tanks of 160,000 cars. It also extracts 70 million ft³ of natural gas per day, enough to provide the total energy used in a year by 1,000 people in the USA.

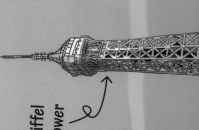

Eiffel Tower

The platform's legs are attached to the seabed and measure

1,755 feet underwater.

The platform is taller than the Eiffel Tower and the Empire State Building.

The legs extend a further

460 feet

down into the seabed, secured in place by deep piles.

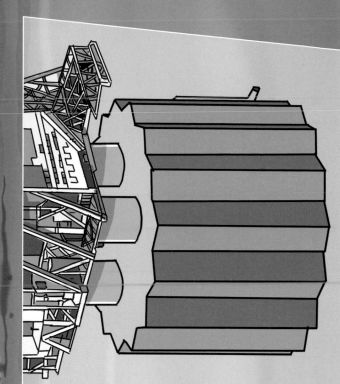

HIBERNIA

While the Petronius is the tallest oil platform in the world, the heaviest platform is the Hibernia in the North Atlantic. The base of the platform is held in place by its massive 660,000-ton weight. This robust design was chosen to ensure that the platform could withstand being hit by an iceberg.

ECO-HOUSE

An eco-house is a house that can run completely self-sufficiently, generating its own electricity and using the resources around it to the maximum extent.

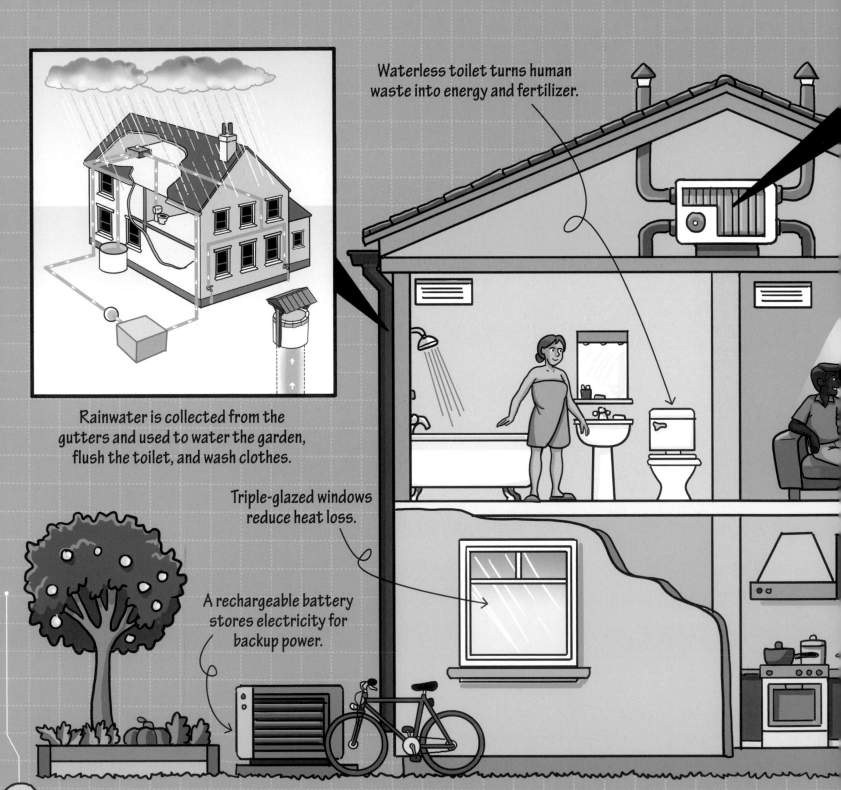

Waterless toilet turns human waste into energy and fertilizer.

Rainwater is collected from the gutters and used to water the garden, flush the toilet, and wash clothes.

Triple-glazed windows reduce heat loss.

A rechargeable battery stores electricity for backup power.

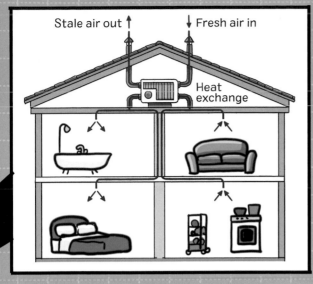

Air ventilation system extracts heat from stale air before expelling it outside.

Stale air out ↑   ↓ Fresh air in

Heat exchange

SUPERTREES

As part of making the city more green, Singapore has created a canopy of artificial trees up to 160 feet high. Eighteen solar-powered Supertrees act as vertical gardens, generating electricity and collecting rainwater for a nearby park. Many high-rise buildings in Singapore now feature trees and smaller plants growing on them.

Insulated roof and walls

Solar panels on a roof that faces the south in the Northern Hemisphere or north in the Southern Hemisphere. These provide the house with most of its electricity.

A geothermal heat pump takes heat from the ground to provide hot water.

FAILED BUILDINGS

When building large structures, if you get the engineering slightly wrong, the results can be disastrous.

LEANING TOWER

Construction of the Tower of Pisa in Italy was started in 1172. The tower began to sink on one side six years into the building work. Its 10-foot foundations were not deep enough to keep it vertical in the soft ground it is built on. Following a pause of 100 years, the tower's construction was completed in spite of the lean. By 1990, the tilt had reached an angle of 5.5 degrees, and it was about to topple over. After work on its foundations, today the 183-foot-tall building tilts at a more stable angle of 4 degrees.

CRACKED TOWER

When the 60-story John Hancock Tower in Boston, Massachusetts, was nearly completed in 1972, glass started to mysteriously fall out of its windows. A few months later, several thousand windows had broken. The tower's design had been tested in a wind tunnel, and engineers were initially confused as to why this was happening. It was eventually discovered that the windows had been fixed in place too rigidly. All 10,334 panes of glass had to be replaced, at a cost of $7 million.

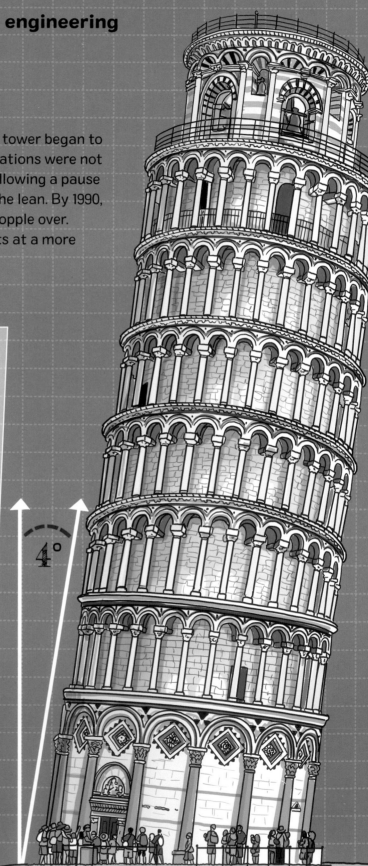

4°

GALLOPING GERTIE

The Tacoma Narrows Bridge, a 1.1-mile-long suspension bridge in Washington, USA, was nicknamed Galloping Gertie by construction workers as the deck was prone to sway wildly in the wind. The bridge was opened to the public in July 1940, but it collapsed just four months later. Strong winds caused the deck to twist violently from side to side until it snapped and fell into the water below. Luckily, nobody was killed. Today, bridge engineers always test their designs in wind tunnels before starting any construction work.

Wind passes through trusses on ordinary bridge.

Wind was forced around trusses on Tacoma Bridge.

On the day of the collapse, wind speeds reached 37 mph. The support cables snapped and the bridge twisted violently from side to side before crumbling into the water below.

DANGEROUS REFLECTIONS

20 Fenchurch Street in London, UK, is also known as the "Walkie-Talkie" as it is shaped like a hand-held radio receiver. Unfortunately, its distinctive shape focuses sunlight onto the streets below. In 2013 while the building was still under construction, a local news reporter fried an egg on the ground using the focused light. A screen had to be installed on the south side of the building to protect people below from the scorching rays.

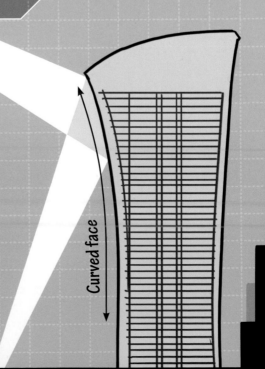

Curved face

ARCHITECTS ON MARS

Some scientists dream of a day when humans are living on Mars. On top of the problem of getting people there, building on Mars presents many difficulties. The climate on Mars is much colder than Earth, there is almost no oxygen to breathe in its thin atmosphere, and the surface is bombarded by deadly radiation. Any human colony would need to be well protected!

GENESIS V.2

Genesis V.2 is a design for a colony on Mars. The donut-shaped base station would sit in a natural crater, protecting the lower levels from the harsh weather conditions on the surface. Everything needed to survive on Mars would be produced inside the base station, including algae farmed for biofuel. Turkish architects Burak Celik, Zeynep Ege Odabasi, and Naz Kaplan imagine that part of the station would be run by robots, with living space for humans alongside.

A tough exterior shell would protect the colony from harmful solar radiation.

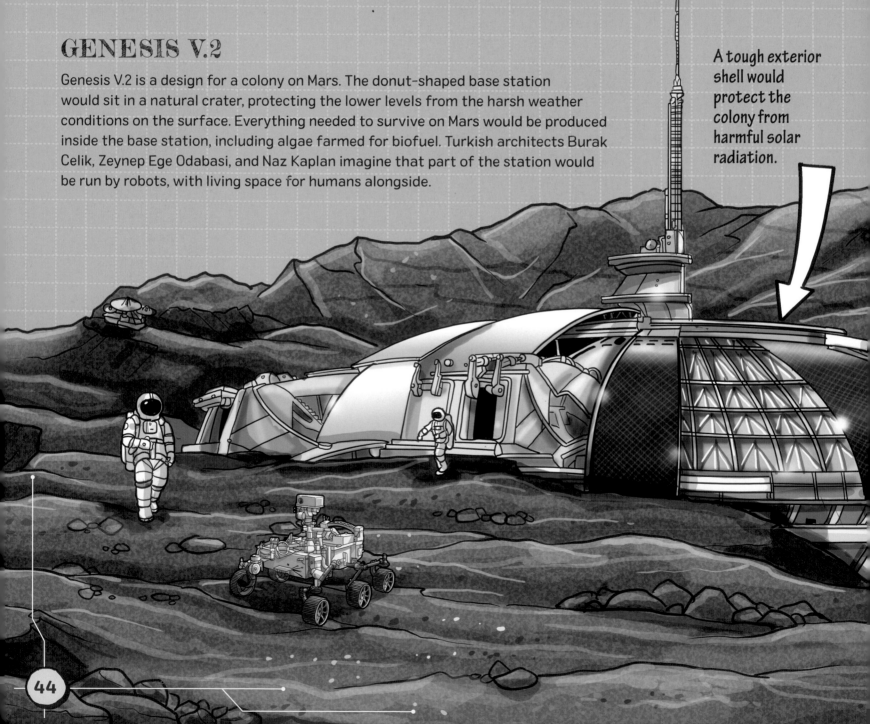

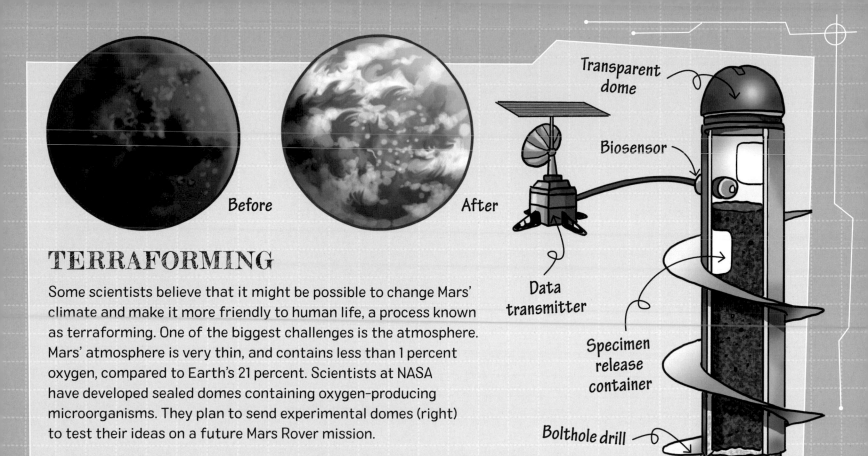

Before

After

Transparent dome

Biosensor

Data transmitter

Specimen release container

Bolthole drill

TERRAFORMING

Some scientists believe that it might be possible to change Mars' climate and make it more friendly to human life, a process known as terraforming. One of the biggest challenges is the atmosphere. Mars' atmosphere is very thin, and contains less than 1 percent oxygen, compared to Earth's 21 percent. Scientists at NASA have developed sealed domes containing oxygen-producing microorganisms. They plan to send experimental domes (right) to test their ideas on a future Mars Rover mission.

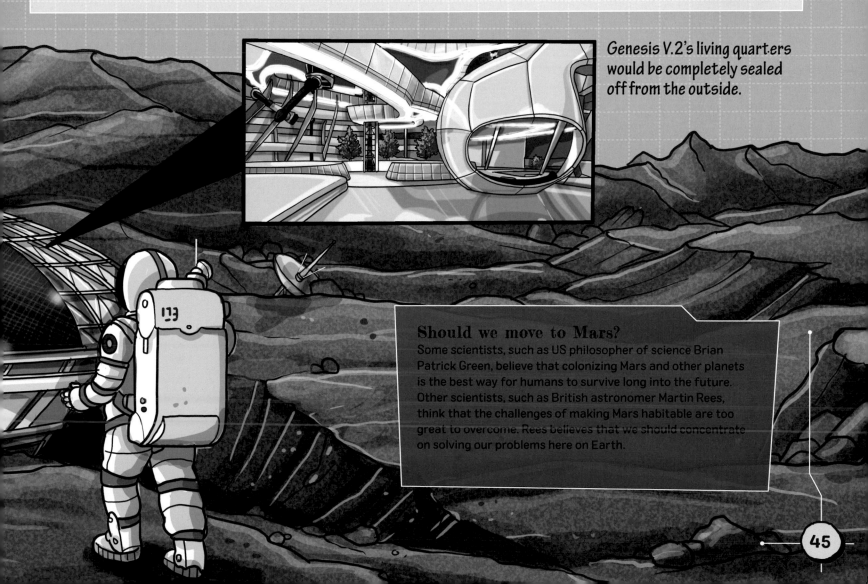

Genesis V.2's living quarters would be completely sealed off from the outside.

Should we move to Mars?

Some scientists, such as US philosopher of science Brian Patrick Green, believe that colonizing Mars and other planets is the best way for humans to survive long into the future. Other scientists, such as British astronomer Martin Rees, think that the challenges of making Mars habitable are too great to overcome. Rees believes that we should concentrate on solving our problems here on Earth.

GLOSSARY

acoustics
The qualities of a building or space that affect the way sounds are transmitted inside it.

air conditioning
A system for controlling the humidity and temperature of the air inside a building, typically used to cool the air in hot climates.

architect
A person who designs buildings and oversees their construction.

bas-relief
A form of sculpture that is carved into a wall. Shapes are raised about an inch from the flat surface to produce a three-dimensional effect.

cable-stayed bridge
A bridge whose deck is held up by diagonal cables attached directly to one or more towers.

civil engineer
A person who designs, builds, and maintains large structures such as buildings, bridges, and tunnels.

deck
The surface of a bridge that carries the roadway, railway or walkway.

foundations
The part of a building that is in direct contact with the ground. The foundations distribute the weight of the building evenly to give it a firm base.

generator
A machine that turns mechanical energy, such as the energy in a turbine, into electricity.

hydraulic
Powered by a moving liquid placed under pressure.

insulate
To cover something with a material that stops heat or sound from being transmitted through it.

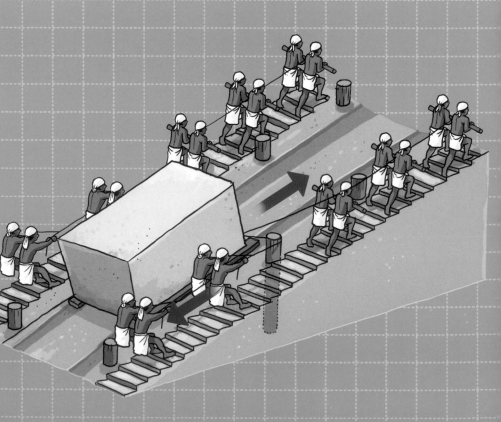

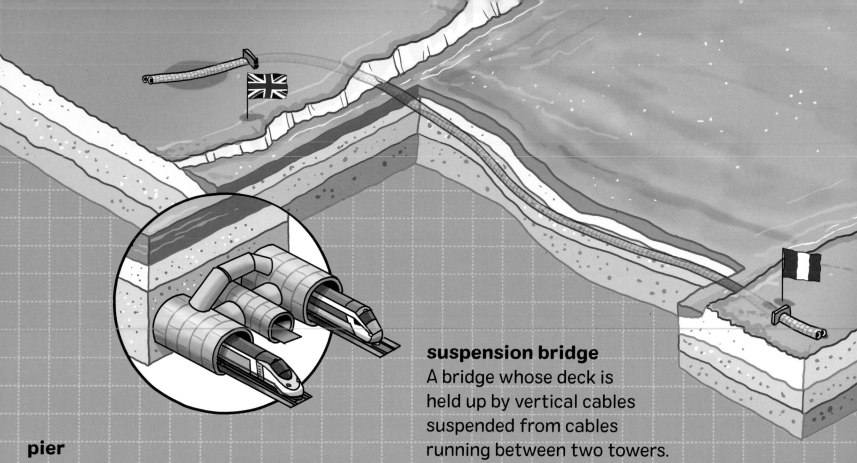

pier
An upright support for a bridge.

pile
A long cylinder made of a strong material such as concrete that is driven into the ground to support a building above it.

solar panel
A device that changes energy from the Sun into electricity.

solar radiation
Energy given off by the Sun in the form of electromagnetic rays.

stone mason
A skilled worker who cuts and prepares stone to make buildings.

strait
A narrow passage of water that connects two larger areas of water.

suspension bridge
A bridge whose deck is held up by vertical cables suspended from cables running between two towers.

terraforming
A process that has been proposed to transform a planet such as Mars so that it resembles Earth and can support life.

tuned mass damper
A device fitted near the top of tall buildings to reduce the amount that the buildings sway from side to side.

turbine
A machine that uses a moving stream of air, water, or steam to turn a shaft. This powers a generator to make electricity.

wind tunnel
A large tube through which air is blown. Scale models of buildings are placed in wind tunnels to study the way that air flows around them.

INDEX